Tomorrow

Lyric by MARTIN CHARNIN
Music by CHARLES STROUSE

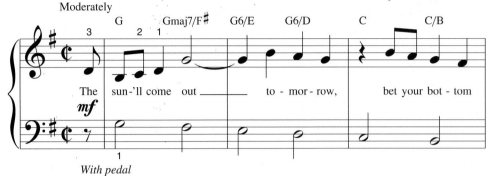

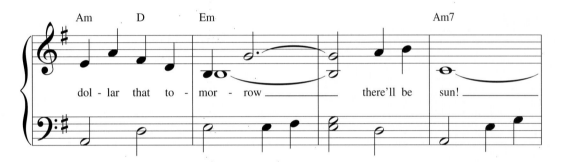

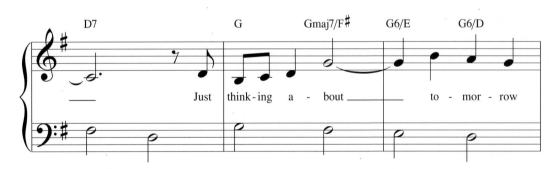

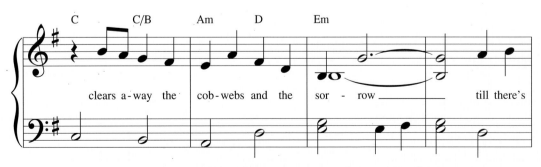

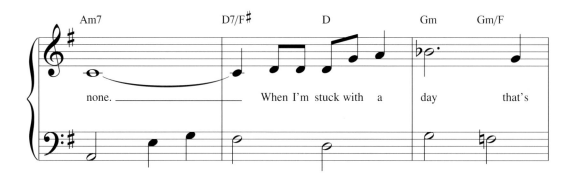

none. _____ When I'm stuck with a day that's

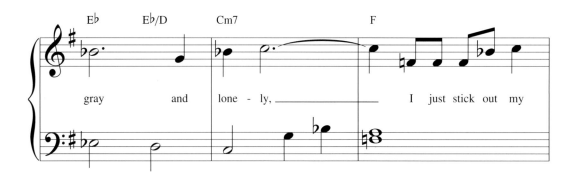

gray and lone - ly, _____ I just stick out my

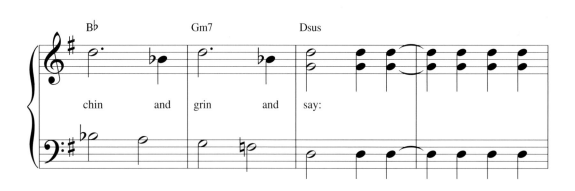

chin and grin and say:

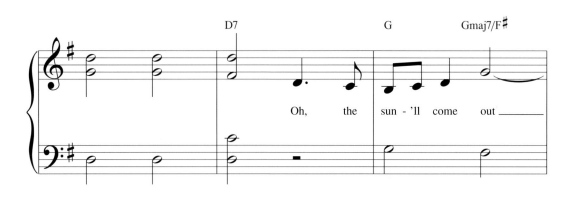

Oh, the sun - 'll come out _____

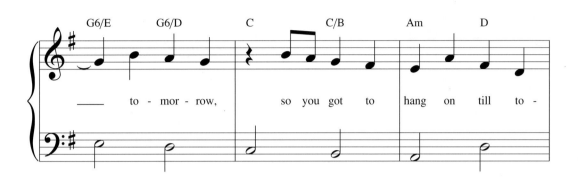

_____ to - mor - row,_   _so you got to_   _hang on till to -_

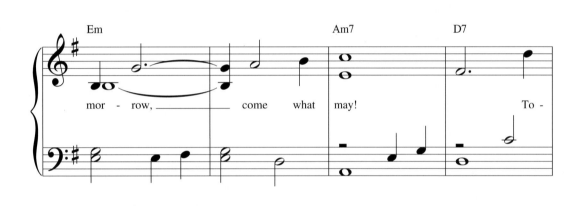

_mor - row, _____ come what may!_   _To -_

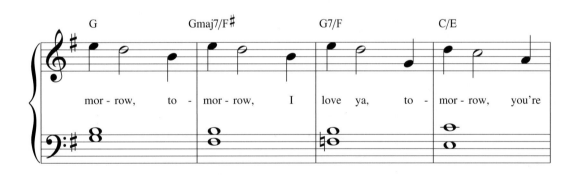

mor - row,   _to - mor - row,_   _I love ya,_   _to - mor - row,_   _you're_

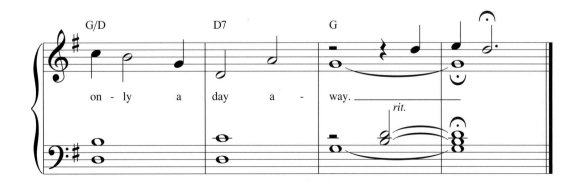

_on - ly a day a - way. _____

You're Never Fully Dressed Without a Smile

Lyric by MARTIN CHARNIN
Music by CHARLES STROUSE

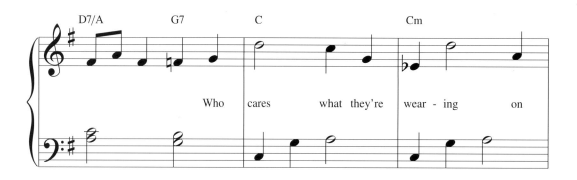

Who cares what they're wear - ing on

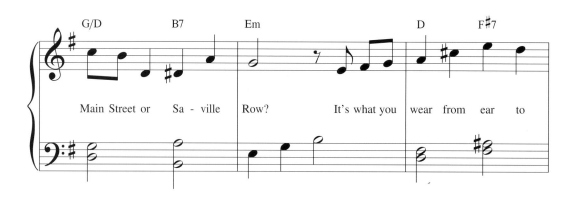

Main Street or Sa - ville Row? It's what you wear from ear to

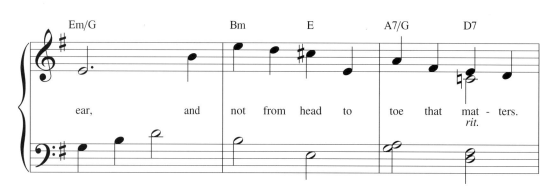

ear, and not from head to toe that mat - ters. *rit.*

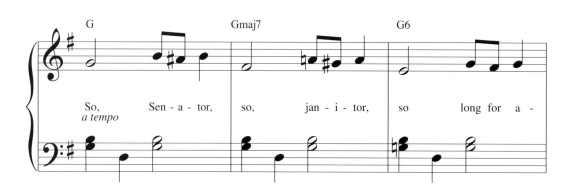

a tempo

So, Sen - a - tor, so, jan - i - tor, so long for a -

A CHORUS LINE

Set on Broadway at an audition for chorus dancers, *A Chorus Line* proves to be a serious and absorbing look at the dancer's life, interpreted through a series of monologues, dialogues, and musical sequences. In 1983, *A Chorus Line* became the longest-running musical in Broadway history.

ONE

Music by MARVIN HAMLISCH
Lyric by EDWARD KLEBAN

Moderately

One
sin - gu - lar sen - sa - tion

ev - 'ry lit - tle step she takes.

One
thrill - ing com - bi - na - tion

ev - 'ry move that she makes.
One smile and

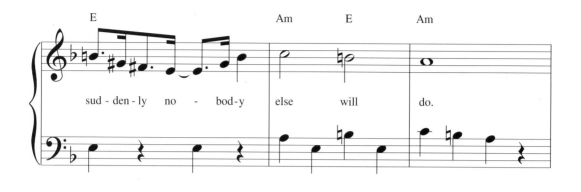

sud - den - ly   no - bod-y   else   will   do.

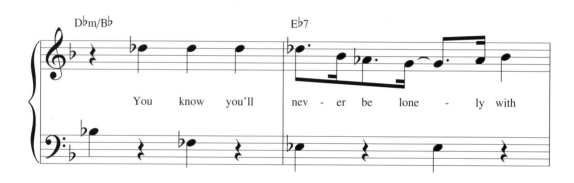

You   know   you'll   nev - er   be   lone - ly   with

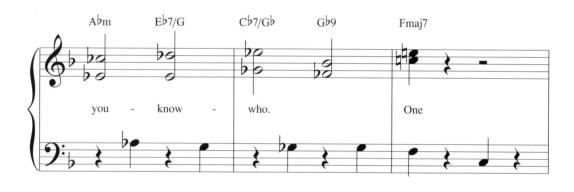

you - know - who.   One

mo - ment in   her pres - ence   and   you can   for - get   the   rest, __

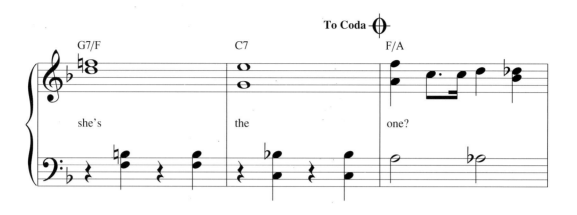

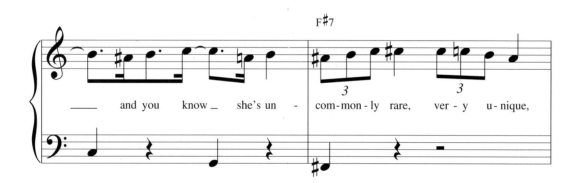

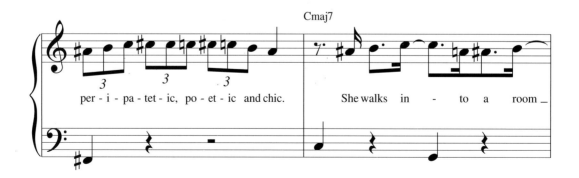

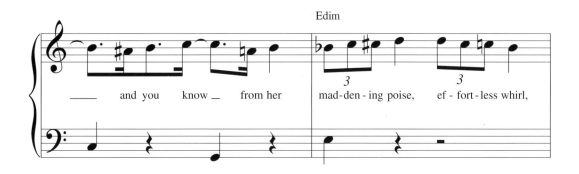

___ and you know _ from her mad-den-ing poise, ef-fort-less whirl,_

she's the spe-cial girl. Stroll - ing,

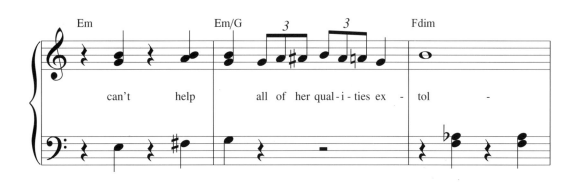

can't help all of her qual-i-ties ex - tol -

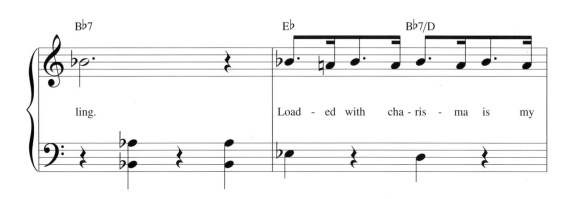

ling. Load - ed with cha-ris-ma is my

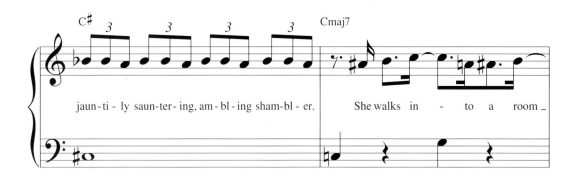

jaun-ti - ly saun-ter- ing, am- bl- ing sham-bl - er. She walks in - to a room _

_ and you know _ you must shuf - fle a - long, join the pa - rade.

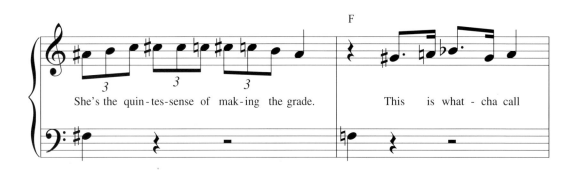

She's the quin - tes-sense of mak - ing the grade. This is what - cha call

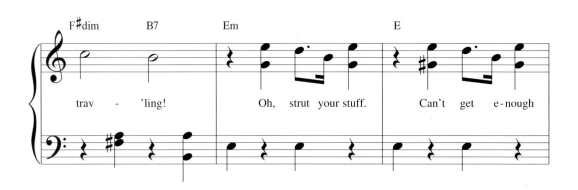

trav - 'ling! Oh, strut your stuff. Can't get e -nough

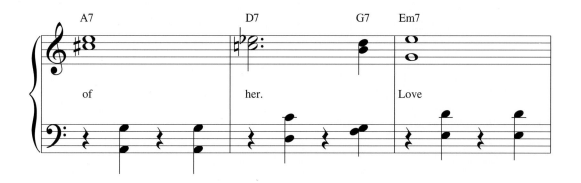

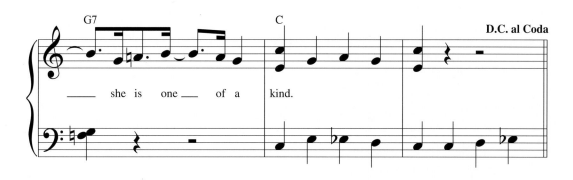

WHAT I DID FOR LOVE

Music by MARVIN HAMLISCH
Lyric by EDWARD KLEBAN

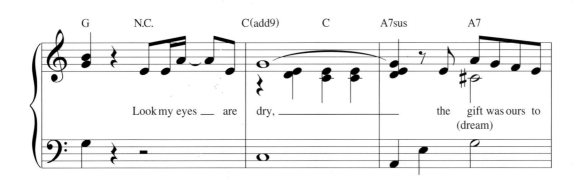

Look my eyes __ are dry, _____ the gift was ours to
(dream)

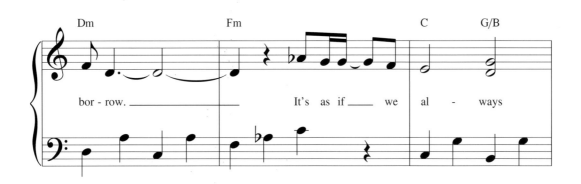

bor - row. _____ It's as if __ we al - ways

knew, but I won't for - get what I did for love, _

_____ what I did for love.

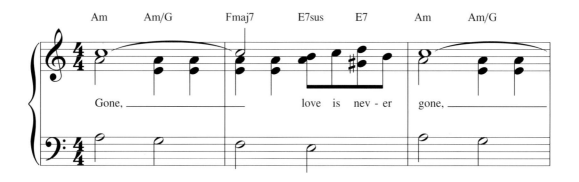

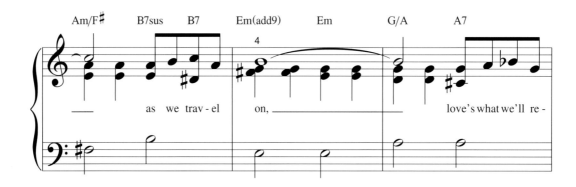

Fiddler on the Roof

A Broadway theatre classic, *Fiddler on the Roof* tells the story of a Jewish community in Czarist Russia as they struggle to maintain their traditions and identities in the face of persecution. Set in the village of Anatevka in 1905, Tevye, a dairyman, his wife Golde, and their five daughters cope with the realities of a harsh life. At the play's end, when a pogrom has forced everyone out of the village, Tevye and what is left of his family look forward to a new life in America.

Sunrise, Sunset

Words by SHELDON HARNICK
Music by JERRY BOCK

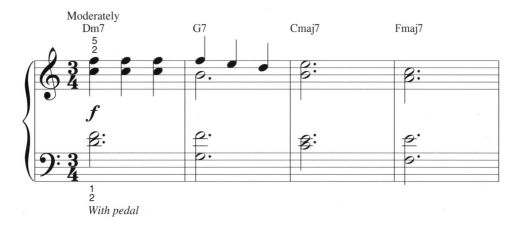

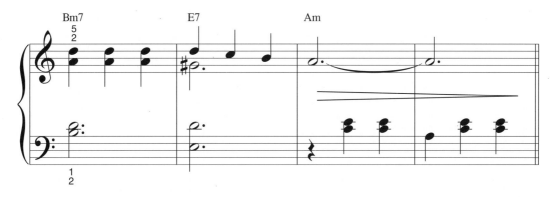

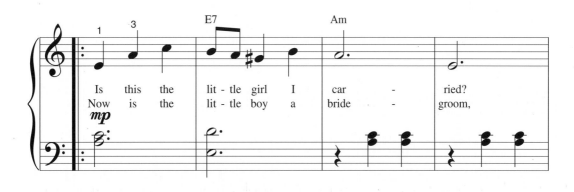

Is this the lit - tle girl I car - ried?
Now is the lit - tle boy a bride - groom,

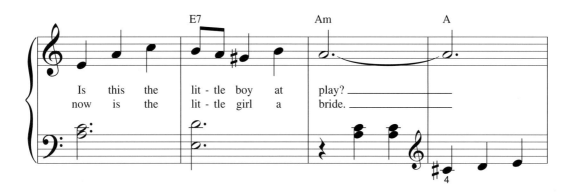

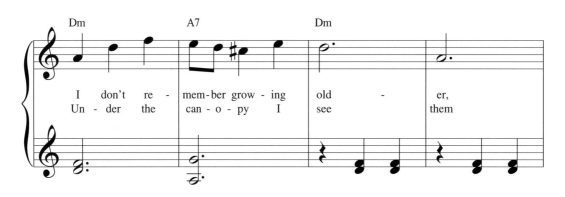

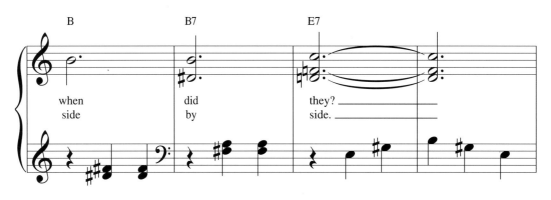

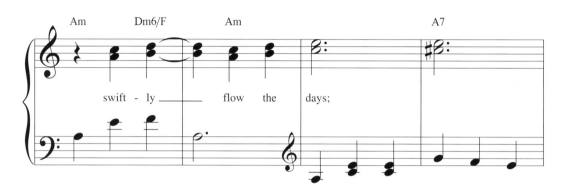

swift - ly ____ flow the days;

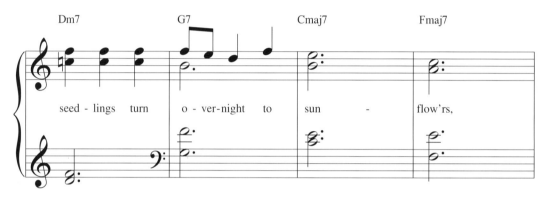

seed - lings turn o - ver-night to sun - flow'rs,

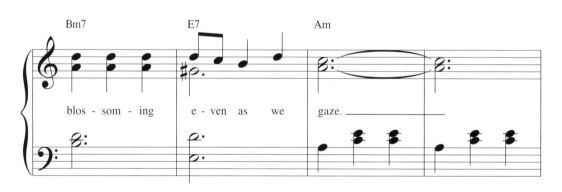

blos - som - ing e - ven as we gaze. ____

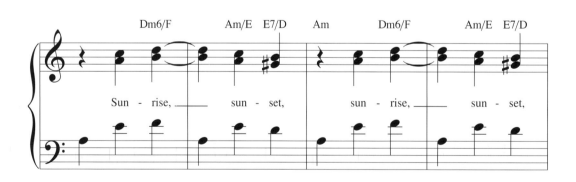

Sun - rise, ____ sun - set, sun - rise, ____ sun - set,

swift - ly ___ fly the years;

one sea - son fol - low - ing an - oth - er,

lad - en with hap - pi - ness and tears.

1.
Am

2.
Am

tears. ___

If I Were a Rich Man

Words by SHELDON HARNICK
Music by JERRY BOCK

Lilting

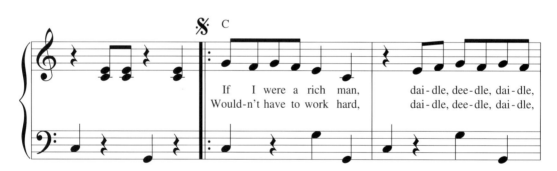

If I were a rich man,
Would-n't have to work hard,

dai - dle, dee - dle, dai - dle,
dai - dle, dee - dle, dai - dle,

dig - guh, dig - guh, dee - dle, dai - dle, dum,
dig - guh, dig - guh, dee - dle, dai - dle, dum,

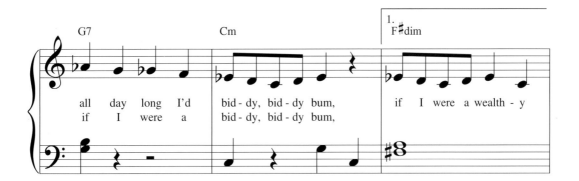

all   day   long   I'd   bid - dy, bid - dy bum,   if   I   were a wealth - y
if   I   were   a   bid - dy, bid - dy bum,

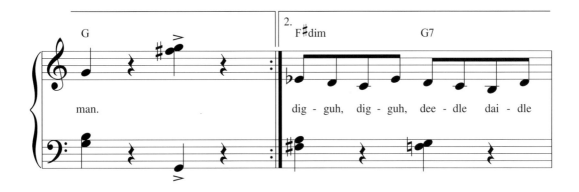

man.   dig - guh, dig - guh, dee - dle dai - dle

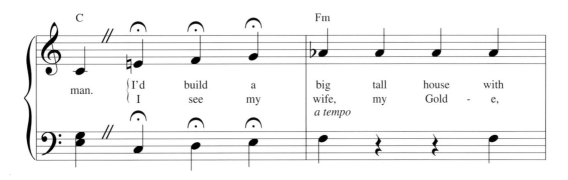

man.   I'd   build   a   big   tall   house   with
         I   see   my   wife,   my   Gold - e,
a tempo

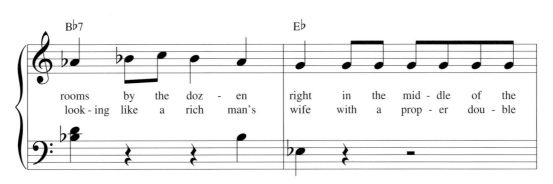

rooms   by   the   doz - en   right   in   the mid - dle of   the
look - ing like a rich man's   wife with a prop - er dou - ble

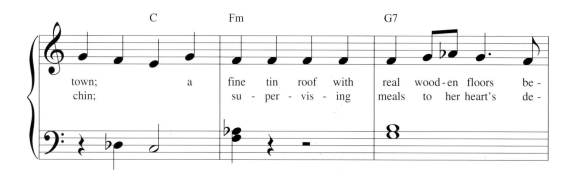

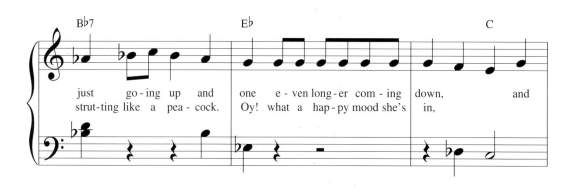

I'd fill my yard with chicks and tur - keys and geese and

mf

a tempo

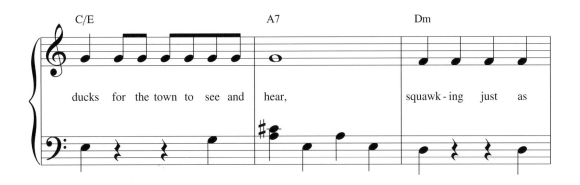

ducks for the town to see and hear, squawk - ing just as

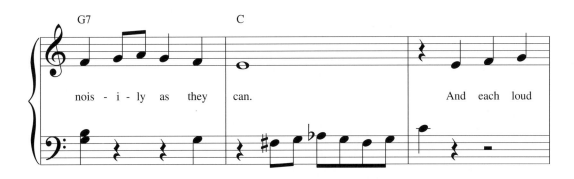

nois - i - ly as they can. And each loud

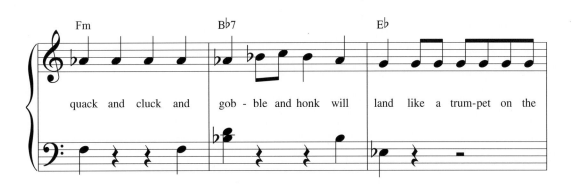

quack and cluck and gob - ble and honk will land like a trum-pet on the

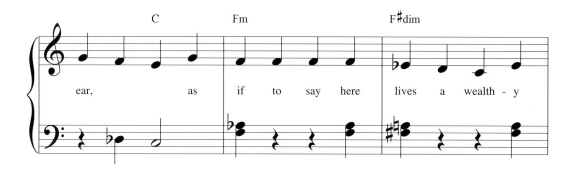

C **Fm** **F♯dim**

ear,   as   if   to   say   here   lives   a   wealth - y

D.S. al Coda
(with repeat)   **CODA**

G

man. _____
rit.

C

If   I   were   a   rich   man,   dai - dle,   dee - dle,   dai - dle,
Would - n't have to work   hard,   dai - dle,   dee - dle,   dai - dle,
a tempo

dig - guh,   dig - guh,   dee - dle,   dai - dle,   dum,
dig - guh,   dig - guh,   dee - dle,   dai - dle,   dum.

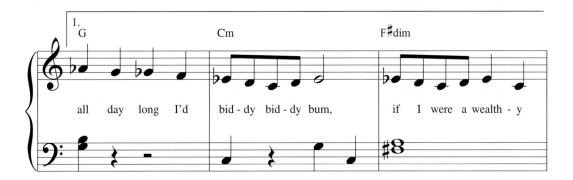

all day long I'd — bid-dy bid-dy bum, — if I were a wealth-y

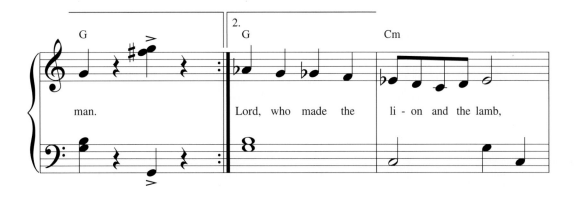

man. — Lord, who made the li-on and the lamb,

you de-creed I should be what I am. Would it spoil some

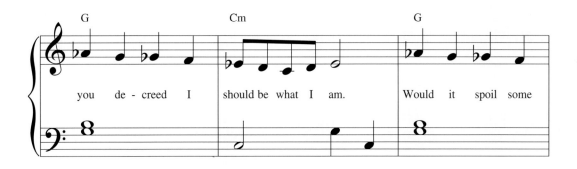

vast e-ter-nal plan, if I were a wealth-y man?

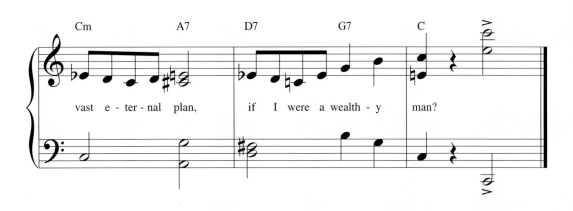

Grease

The story of hip Danny Duke and his wholesome girl, Sandy Dumbrowski, serves as the centerpiece for this light-hearted recreation of the rock 'n' rolling 1950s. After a highly successful Broadway engagement, *Grease* became one of the biggest film musicals in recent history, and for a time (until being overtaken by *A Chorus Line*), it was the longest-running show in Broadway history.

Beauty School Dropout

Lyric and Music by WARREN CASEY
and JIM JACOBS

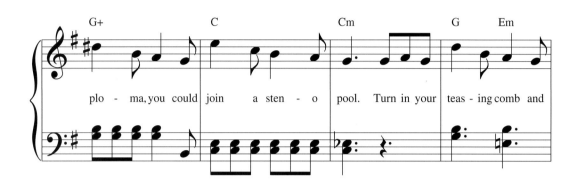

plo - ma, you could join a sten - o pool. Turn in your teas - ing comb and

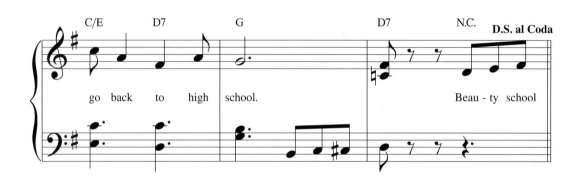

D.S. al Coda

go back to high school. Beau - ty school

CODA

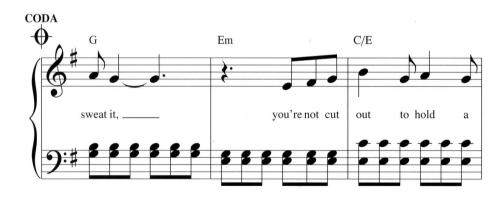

sweat it, _____ you're not cut out to hold a

job. _____ Bet - ter for - get it; _____ who wants their

We Go Together

Lyric and Music by WARREN CASEY
and JIM JACOBS

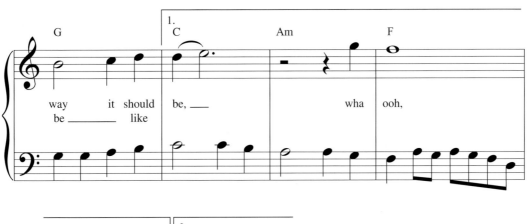

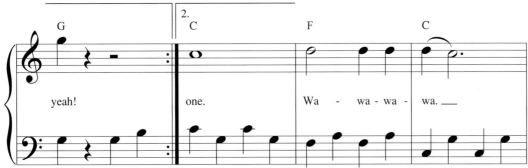

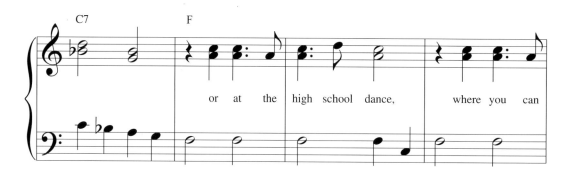

or at the high school dance, where you can

find ro-mance, may-be it might be love. _____

_____ We're for each oth - er like-a wop ba-ba lu-mop and

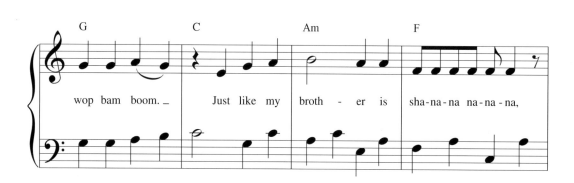

wop bam boom. _ Just like my broth - er is sha-na-na na-na-na,

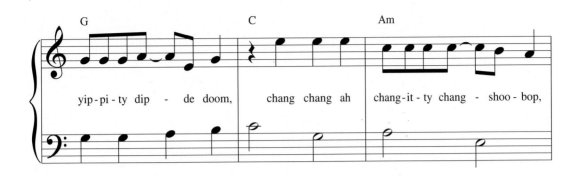

yip - pi - ty dip - de doom,   chang chang ah   chang - it - ty chang - shoo - bop,

we'll   al - ways   be _____ to - geth - er, _____

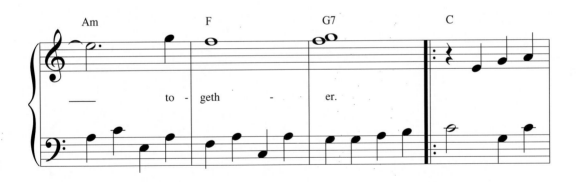

_____ to - geth - er.

GUYS and DOLLS

This "Musical Fable of Broadway" tells the tale of how Miss Sarah Brown of the Save-a-Soul Mission saves the souls of assorted Times Square riffraff while losing her heart to the smooth-talking gambler, Sky Masterson. A more comic romance involves Nathan Detroit, who runs the "oldest established permanent floating crap game in New York," and Miss Adelaide, the star of the Hot Box nightclub, to whom he has been engaged for fourteen years. Abe Burrows' libretto and Frank Loesser's perfectly fitting score make this an accepted theatrical classic.

I'VE NEVER BEEN IN LOVE BEFORE

By FRANK LOESSER

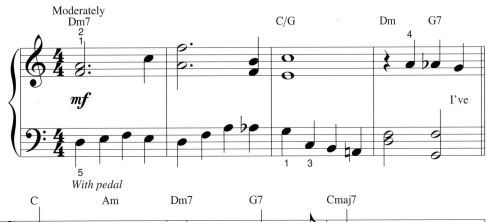

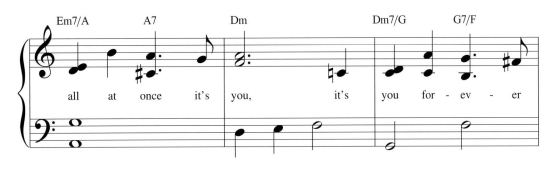

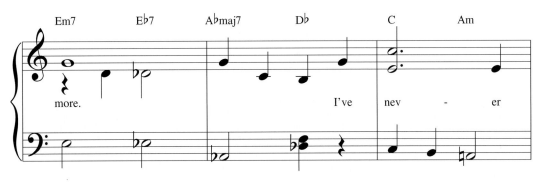

been in love be - fore. I thought my heart was

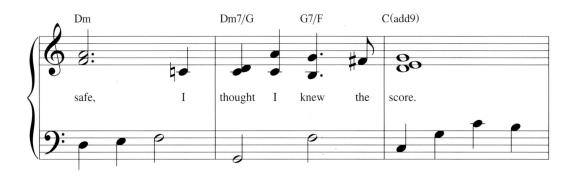

safe, I thought I knew the score.

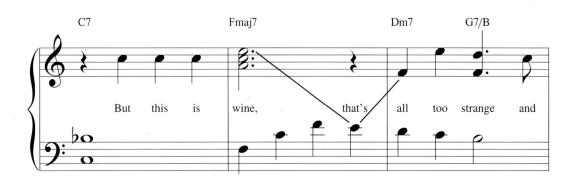

But this is wine, that's all too strange and

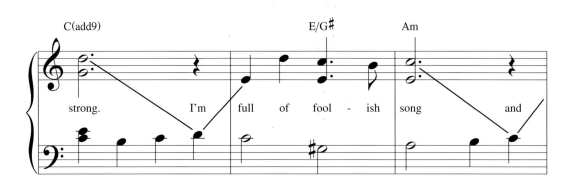

strong. I'm full of fool - ish song and

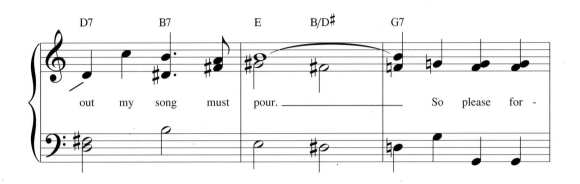

out my song must pour. _____ So please for -

give this help - less haze I'm in; I've

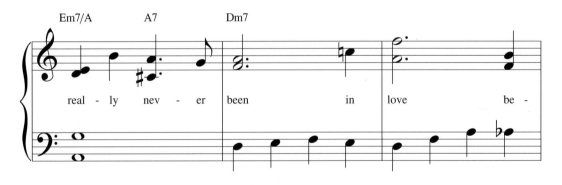

real - ly nev - er been in love be -

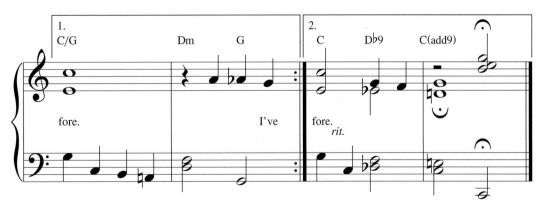

fore. I've fore.
rit.

LUCK BE A LADY

By FRANK LOESSER

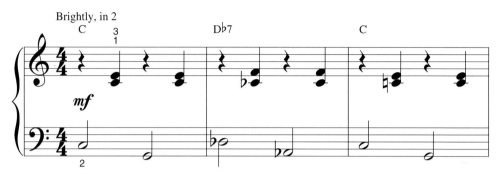

Luck if you've ev - er been a la - dy to be -

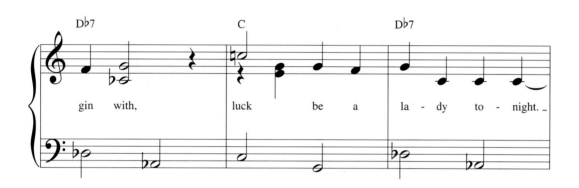

gin with, luck be a la - dy to - night.

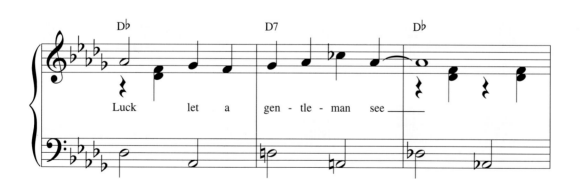

Luck let a gen - tle - man see

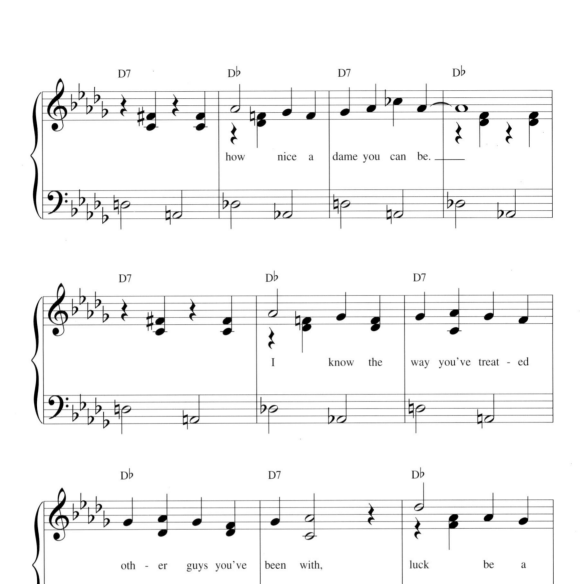

how   nice   a   dame you can be._____

I   know the   way you've treat - ed

oth - er guys you've been with,   luck   be   a

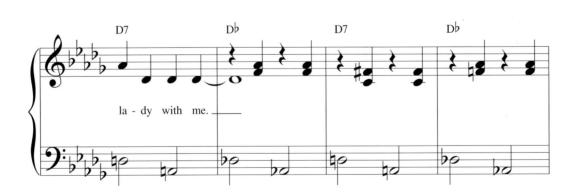

la - dy with me._____

A la - dy does - n't leave her

es - cort. It is - n't fair! It is - n't

nice! A la - dy does - n't wan - der all

o - ver the room and blow on some

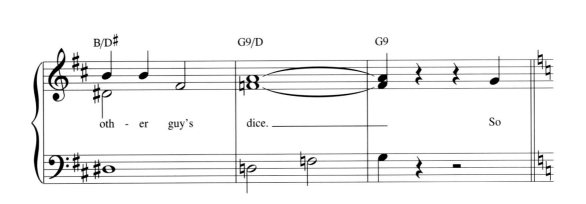

oth - er guy's dice. _____ So

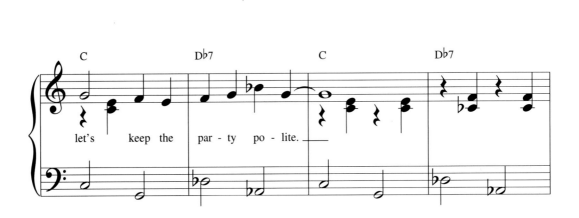

let's keep the par - ty po - lite. _____

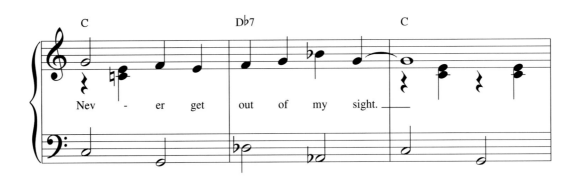

Nev - er get out of my sight. _____

Stick with me, ba - by, I'm the

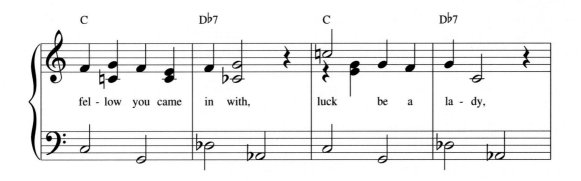

fel - low you came   in with,   luck   be   a   la - dy,

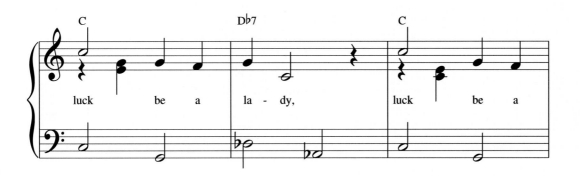

luck   be   a   la - dy,   luck   be   a

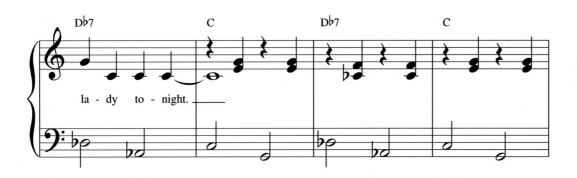

la - dy   to - night.

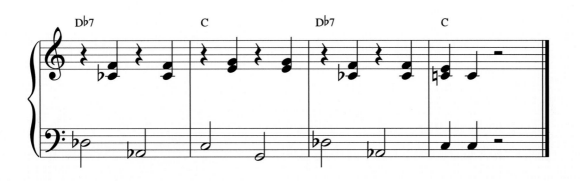

The King and I

Based on the diaries of an adventurous Englishwoman, *The King and I* is set in Bangkok in the early 1860s. Anna Leonowens, the schoolteacher to the Siamese king's children, has frequent clashes with the monarch but eventually comes to exert great influence on him, particularly in creating a more democratic society for his people. The show marked the fifth collaboration between Richard Rodgers and Oscar Hammerstein II, and their third to run over one thousand performances.

Getting to Know You

Lyrics by OSCAR HAMMERSTEIN II
Music by RICHARD RODGERS

Moderately

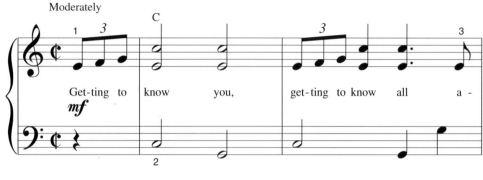

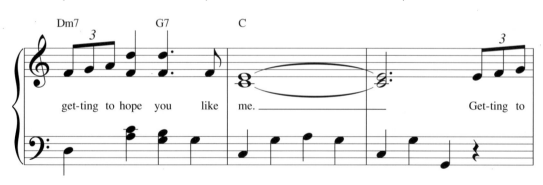

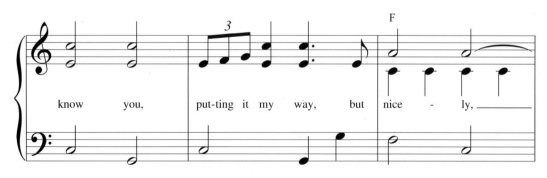

I Whistle a Happy Tune

Lyrics by OSCAR HAMMERSTEIN II
Music by RICHARD RODGERS

When ev-er I feel a-fraid I
whis-tle a hap-py tune and

hold my head e-rect and whis-tle a hap-py
ev-'ry sin-gle time and the hap-pi-ness in the

tune, so no one will sus-pect I'm a-
tune con-vinc-es me that

fraid. While shiv-er-ing in my shoes, I

strike a care - less pose and whis - tle a hap - py

tune and no one ev - er knows I'm a - fraid. _____

_____ The re - sult of this de - cep - tion is

ver - y strange to _____ tell, for when I fool the

Gm6 D9 G7 **D.S. al Coda**

peo - ple I fear, I fool my - self as well! I

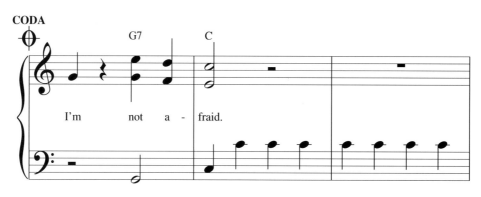

CODA

G7 C

I'm not a - fraid.

F/A C/G

Make be - lieve you're brave and the trick will take you

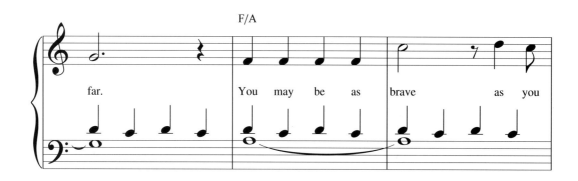

F/A

far. You may be as brave as you

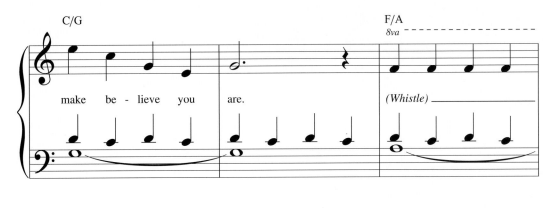

make be - lieve you are.

F/A

(Whistle)

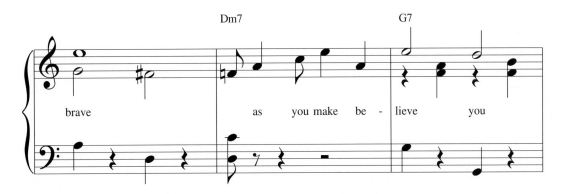

C/G

D7

You may be as

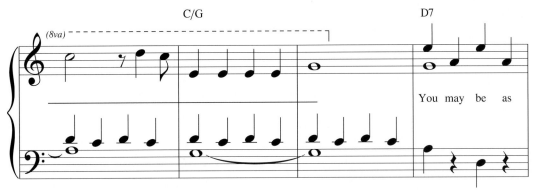

brave

as you make be - lieve you

Dm7

G7

are.

C

3 1

Les Misérables

Victor Hugo's monumental romantic novel is the basis of the show of the same name. The epic story presents the downtrodden and their struggle to survive in nineteenth-century France against the obstacles in a class-structured society. The show was originally written in 1979 and presented in Paris on a relatively small scale. Reconceived into a full-fledged pop opera, it opened in London in 1985 and became one of the biggest successes in Broadway history.

I Dreamed a Dream

Music by CLAUDE-MICHEL SCHÖNBERG
Lyrics by ALAIN BOUBLIL,
JEAN-MARC NATEL and HERBERT KRETZMER

On My Own

Music by CLAUDE-MICHEL SCHÖNBERG
Lyrics by ALAIN BOUBLIL, JEAN-MARC NATEL,
HERBERT KRETZMER, JOHN CAIRD and TREVOR NUNN

THE MUSIC MAN

The Music Man represents the innocent charm of a Middle American town. The show opens on the Fourth of July, 1912, in River City, Iowa, and "Professor" Harold Hill, a traveling salesman of musical instruments, has arrived to con the citizens into believing that he can teach the town's children how to play in a marching band. But instead of skipping town before the instruments are to arrive, Hill remains because of the love of a good woman, librarian Marian Paroo. The story ends with the children, though barely able to produce any kind of recognizable musical sound, celebrated by their proud parents.

GARY, INDIANA

By MEREDITH WILLSON

Soft Shoe Bounce

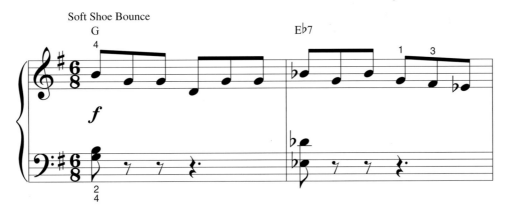

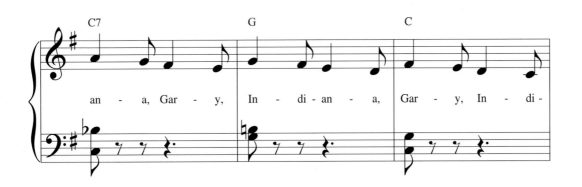

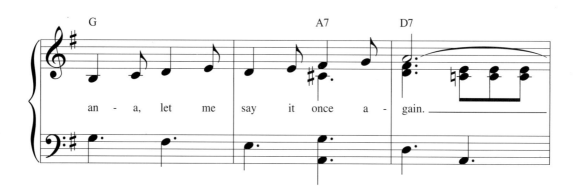

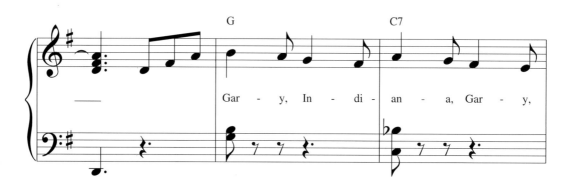

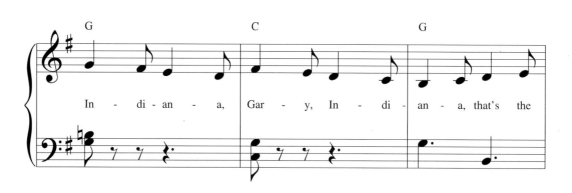

like to have a log - i - cal ex - pla - na - tion

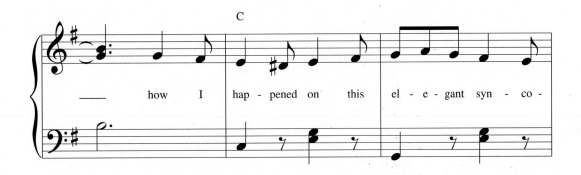

how I hap - pened on this el - e - gant syn - co -

pa - tion, I will say with - out a

mo - ment of hes - i - ta - tion, there is

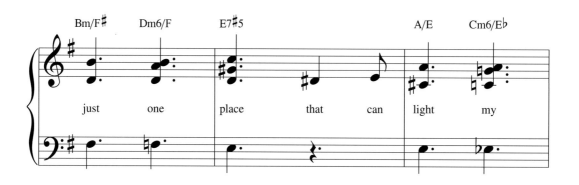

just one place that can light my

face. Gar - y, In - di - an - a, Gar - y,

In - di - an - a, not Lou - is - i - an - a, Par - is,

France, New York or Rome, but

Gar - y, In - di - an - a, Gar - y, In - di - an - a,

Gar - y, In - di - an - a, my home, sweet

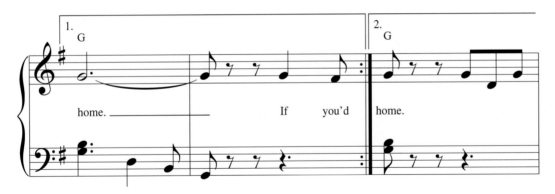

home. _____ If you'd home.

TILL THERE WAS YOU

By MEREDITH WILLSON

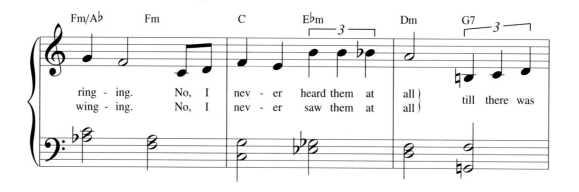

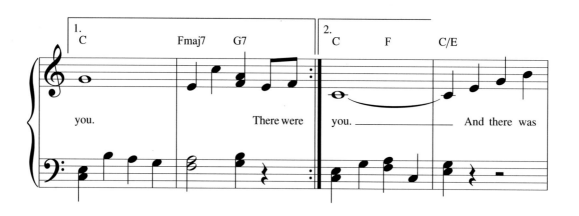

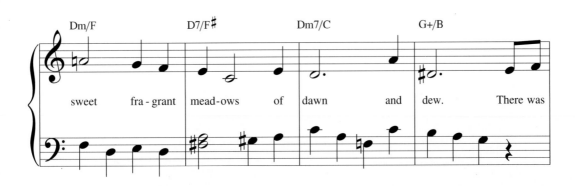

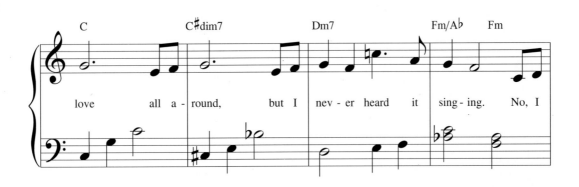

Oklahoma!

Set in Indian Territory soon after the turn of the century, *Oklahoma!* spins a simple tale mostly concerned with whether the decent Curly, or the menacing Jud, gets to take Laurey to the box social. Though she chooses Jud in a fit of annoyance, Laurey really loves Curly and they soon make plans to marry. At their wedding they join in celebrating Oklahoma's impending statehood before riding off in their surrey with the fringe on top. Recognized as a landmark in the history of American musical theatre (and Rodgers and Hammerstein's first collaboration), the show expertly connects the major elements in the production—story, song, and dance, and also uses dream ballets to reveal hidden desires and fears of the main characters.

People Will Say We're in Love

Lyrics by OSCAR HAMMERSTEIN II
Music by RICHARD RODGERS

With a lilt

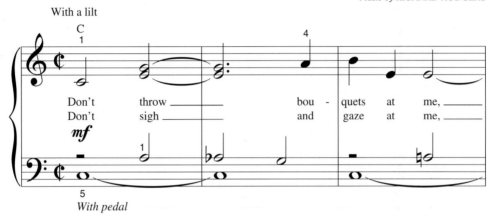

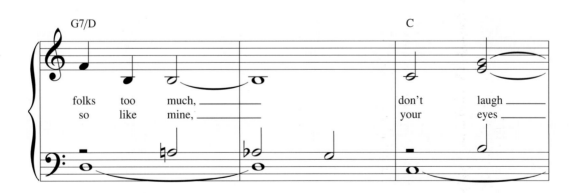

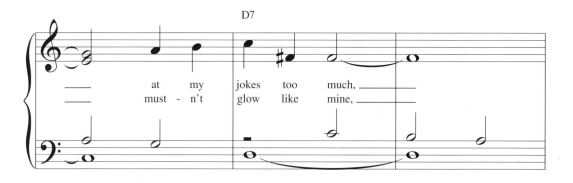

at my   jokes   too   much,
must - n't   glow   like   mine,

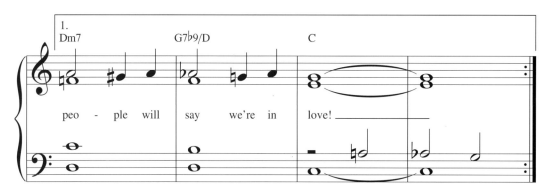

peo - ple will   say   we're in   love!

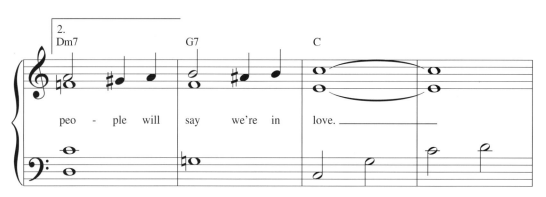

peo - ple will   say   we're in   love.

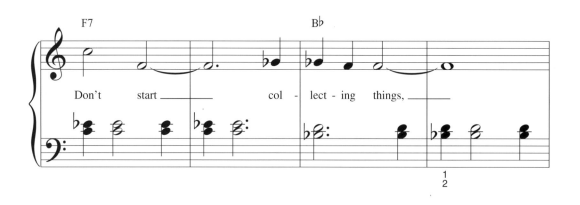

Don't   start   col - lect - ing   things,

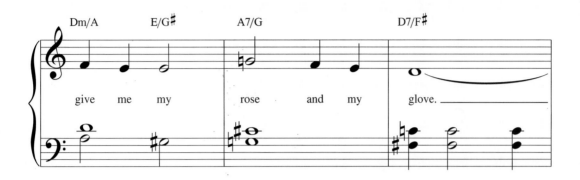

give me my rose and my glove. _____

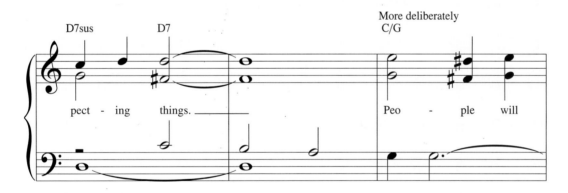

_____ Sweet - heart, _____ they're sus -

pect - ing things. _____

More deliberately

Peo - ple will

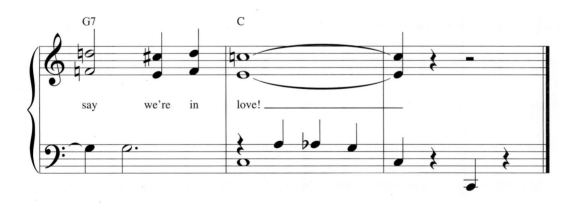

say we're in love! _____

Oklahoma

Lyrics by OSCAR HAMMERSTEIN II
Music by RICHARD RODGERS

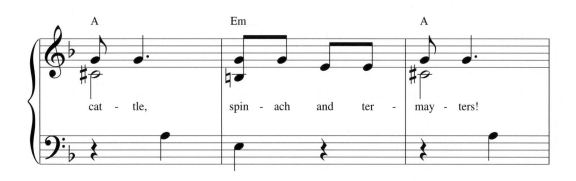

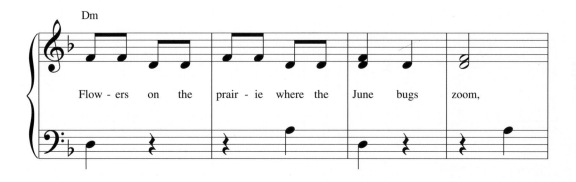

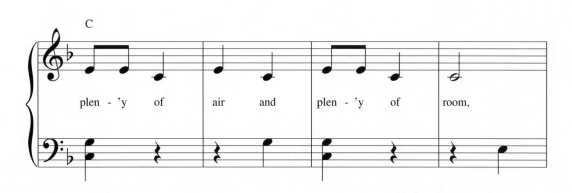

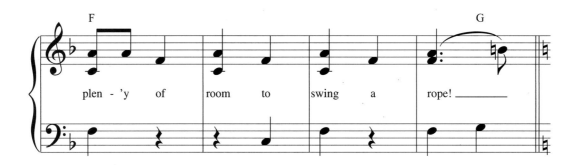

plen - 'y   of   room   to   swing   a   rope! _____

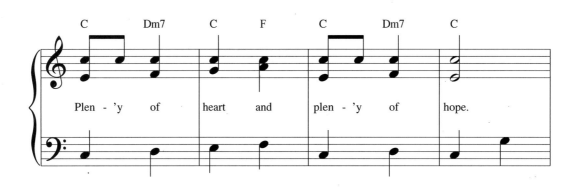

Plen - 'y   of   heart   and   plen - 'y   of   hope.

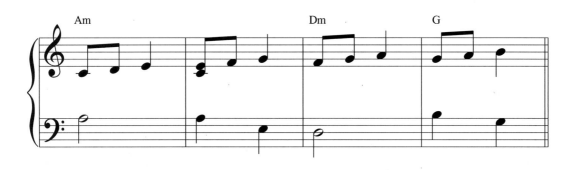

O - - - k - la - ho - ma, where the
O - - - k - la - ho - ma, ev - 'ry

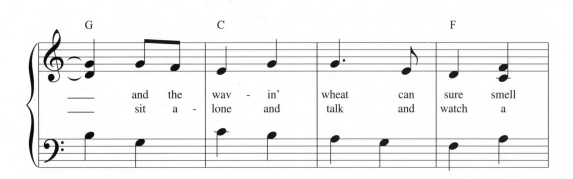

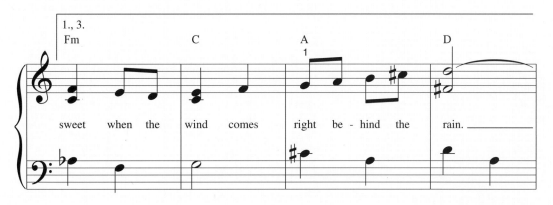

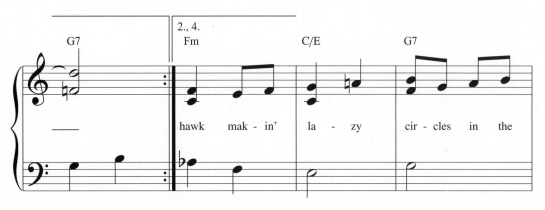

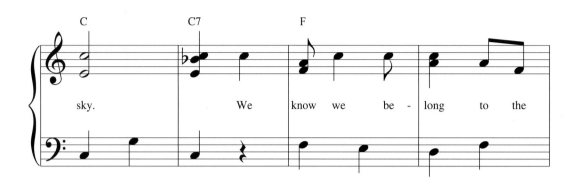

sky.　　　　　We　know　we　be - long　to　the

land _____　　and　the　land　we　be - long　to　is

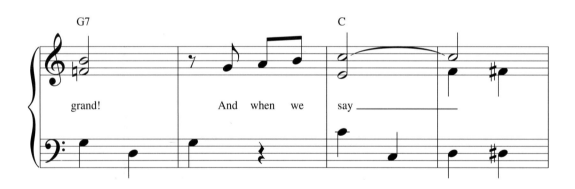

grand!　　　　And　when　we　say _____

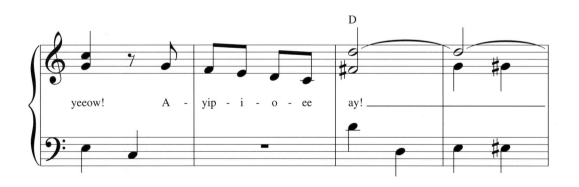

yeeow!　A - yip - i - o - ee　ay! _____

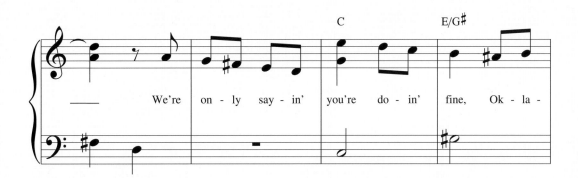

We're on - ly say - in' you're do - in' fine, Ok - la -

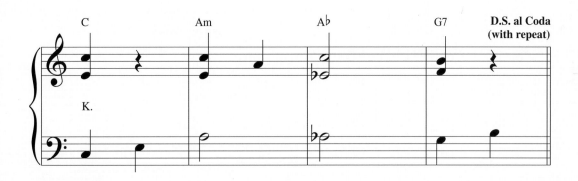

ho - ma! Ok - la - ho - ma _____ O.

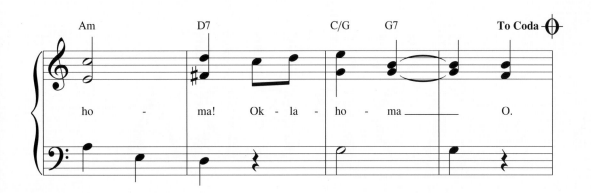

K.

D.S. al Coda
(with repeat)

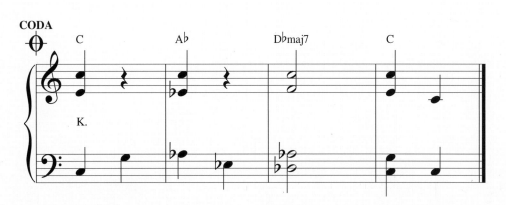

CODA

K.

THE PHANTOM OF THE OPERA

One of the most successful musicals in history is based on the French novel *Le Fantôme de l'Opéra*, first published in 1911. The disfigured phantom lives in the forgotten shadows of the Paris Opera, and falls in love with Christine, for whom he is willing to do anything. He eliminates any rivals, and convinces her of his sincere affection. The production's most famous element is a chandelier that falls from above the audience and crashes onto the stage. *Phantom* has had the most number of touring companies and the most successful road revenues in history.

ALL I ASK OF YOU

Music by ANDREW LLOYD WEBBER
Lyrics by CHARLES HART
Additional Lyrics by RICHARD STILGOE

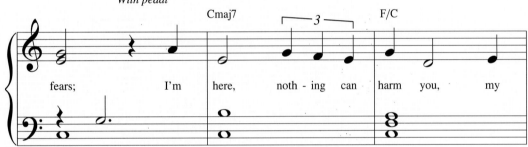

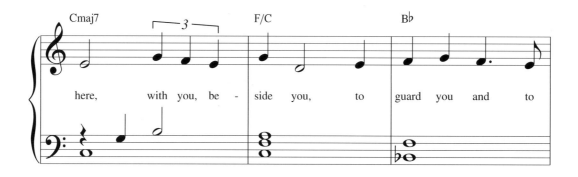

here, with you, be - side you, to guard you and to

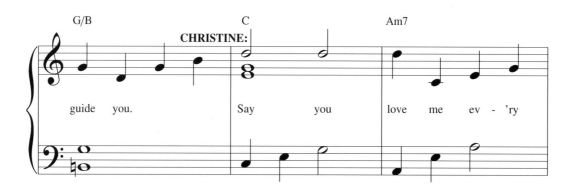

CHRISTINE:

guide you. Say you love me ev - 'ry

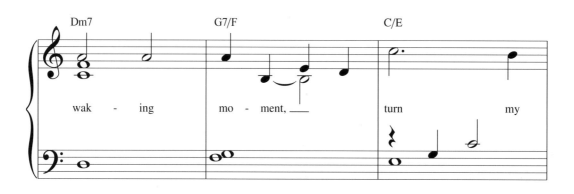

wak - ing mo - ment, ___ turn my

head with talk of sum - mer - time.

C   Am7   Dm7

Say   you   need   me   with   you   now   and

G7/F   C/E   F

al - ways; __   prom - ise   me   that   all   you   say   is

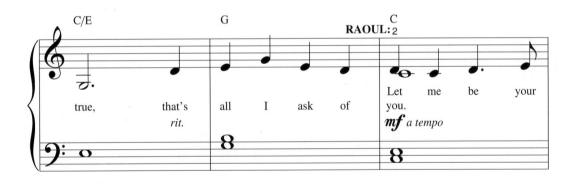

C/E   G   **RAOUL:**   C

true,   that's   all   I   ask   of   Let   me   be   your

rit.   you.   **mf** *a tempo*

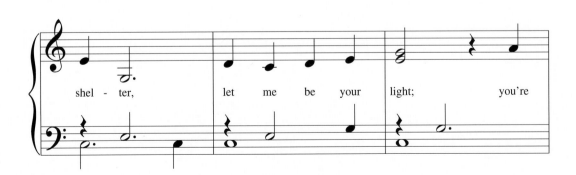

shel - ter,   let   me   be   your   light;   you're

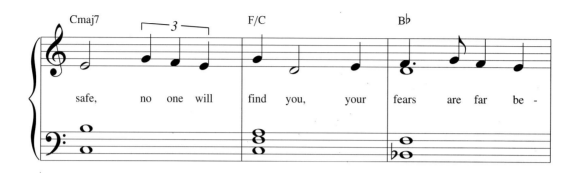

safe, no one will find you, your fears are far be-

CHRISTINE:

hind you. All I want is free - dom, a

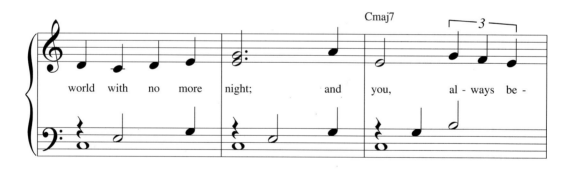

world with no more night; and you, al - ways be -

RAOUL:

side me, to hold me and to hide me. Then

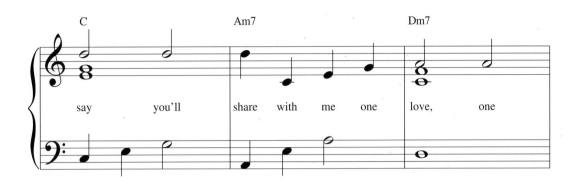

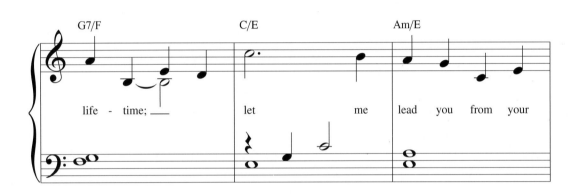

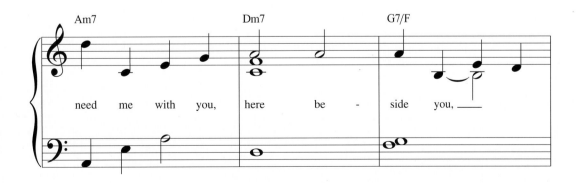

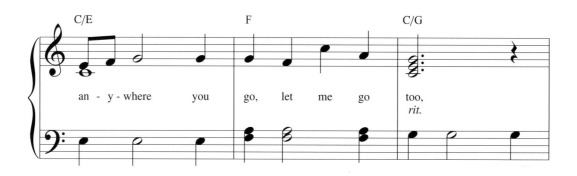

an - y - where you go, let me go too, *rit.*

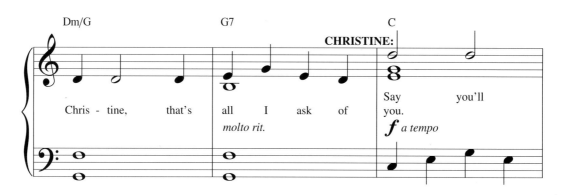

Chris - tine, that's all I ask of you. **CHRISTINE:** Say you'll

molto rit. *f* *a tempo*

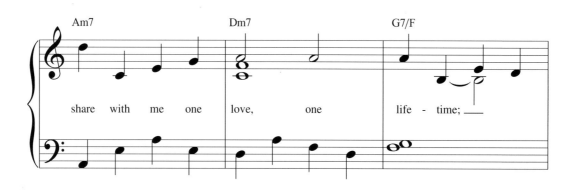

share with me one love, one life - time; ___

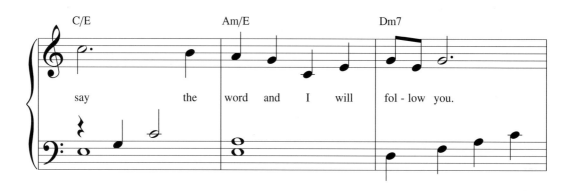

say the word and I will fol - low you.

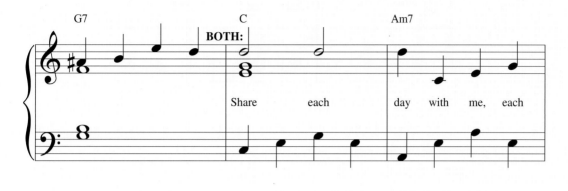

G7   C   Am7

BOTH:

Share   each   day   with   me,   each

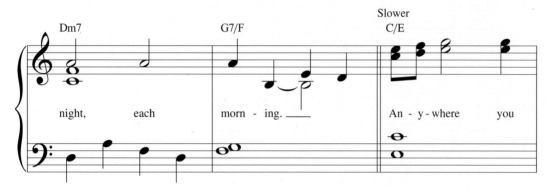

Dm7   G7/F   Slower   C/E

night,   each   morn - ing. ____   An - y - where   you

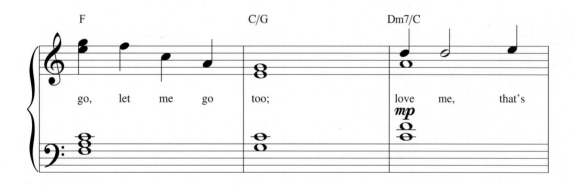

F   C/G   Dm7/C

go,   let   me   go   too;   love   me,   that's

mp

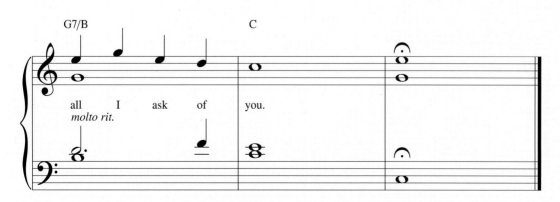

G7/B   C

all   I   ask   of   you.

molto rit.

The Music of the Night

Music by ANDREW LLOYD WEBBER
Lyrics by CHARLES HART
Additional Lyrics by RICHARD STILGOE

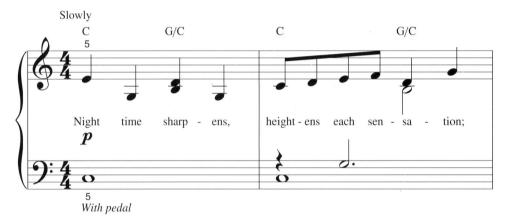

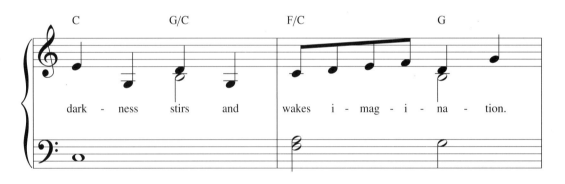

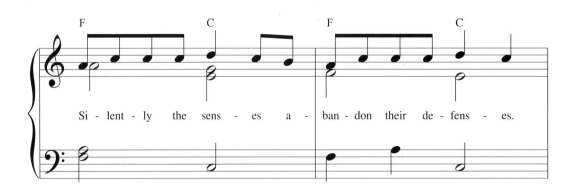

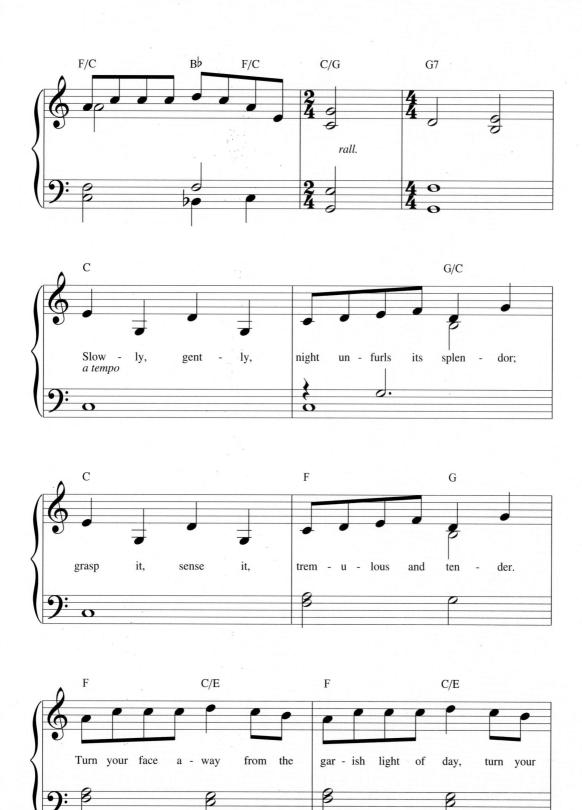

thoughts a - way from cold, un - feel - ing light and

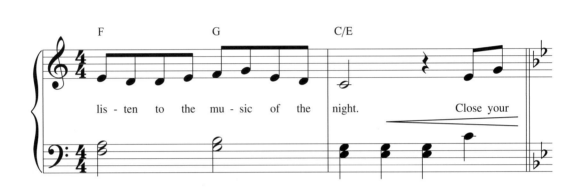

lis - ten to the mu - sic of the night. Close your

eyes and sur - ren - der to your dark - est dreams! Purge your

mp

thoughts of the life you knew be - fore! Close your

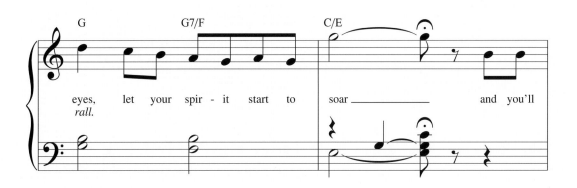

eyes, let your spir-it start to soar _____ and you'll
rall.

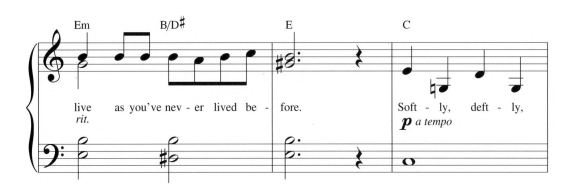

live as you've nev-er lived be-fore.   Soft-ly, deft-ly,
rit.   **p** *a tempo*

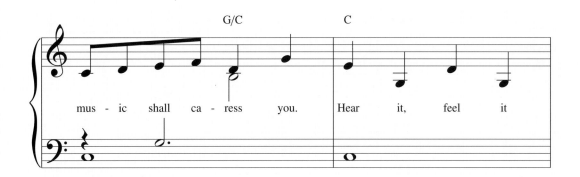

mus-ic shall ca-ress you.   Hear it, feel it

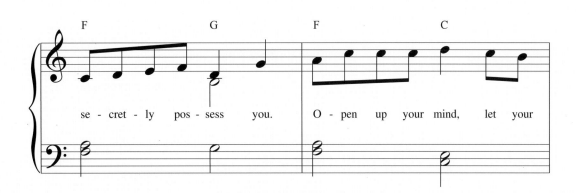

se-cret-ly pos-sess you.   O-pen up your mind, let your

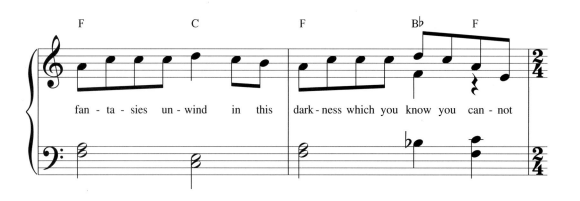

fan - ta - sies un - wind in this dark - ness which you know you can - not

fight, the dark - ness of the mu - sic of the
rit.

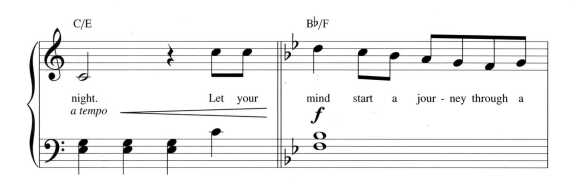

night. Let your mind start a jour - ney through a
a tempo

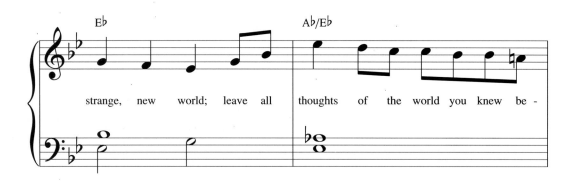

strange, new world; leave all thoughts of the world you knew be -

Let the dream be - gin, let your dark - er side give in to the

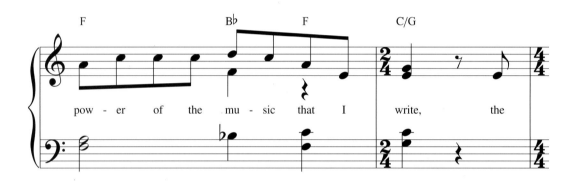

pow - er of the mu - sic that I write, the

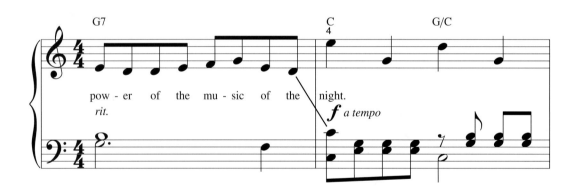

pow - er of the mu - sic of the night.
rit.   *f* *a tempo*

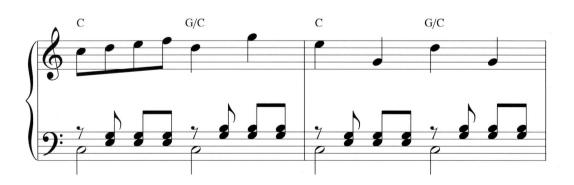

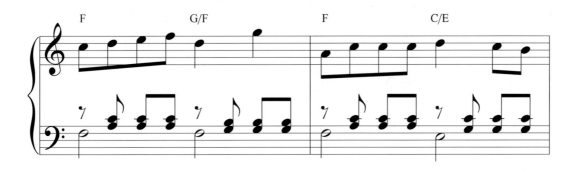

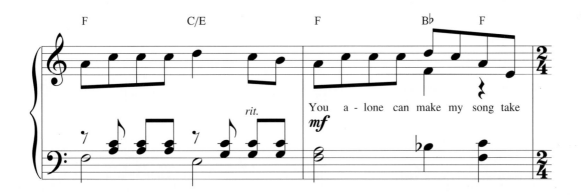

You a - lone can make my song take

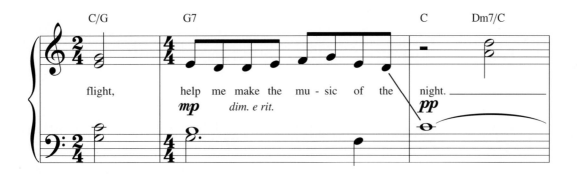

flight, help me make the mu - sic of the night. _____

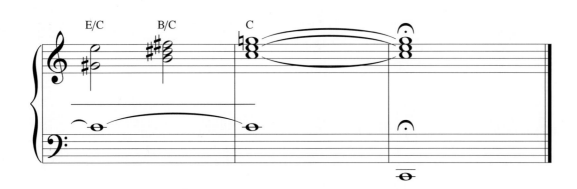

The Sound of Music

The story of *The Sound of Music* was adapted from Maria Von Trapp's autobiographical *The Trapp Family Singers*, and is set in Austria in 1938. Maria Rainier, a free-spirited postulant at Nonnburg Abbey, takes a position as governess to the seven children of the widowed and stern Captain Georg Von Trapp. After Maria and the captain fall in love and marry, their happiness is quickly shattered by the Nazi invasion, which forces the family to flee over the Alps to Switzerland. *The Sound of Music* was Rodgers and Hammerstein's final collaboration and became their third longest-running Broadway production.

Do-Re-Mi

Lyrics by OSCAR HAMMERSTEIN II
Music by RICHARD RODGERS

Lively

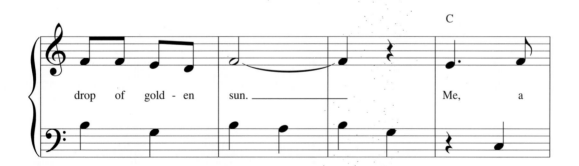

Tea,   a   drink   with   jam   and   bread

that   will   bring   us   back   to   do.

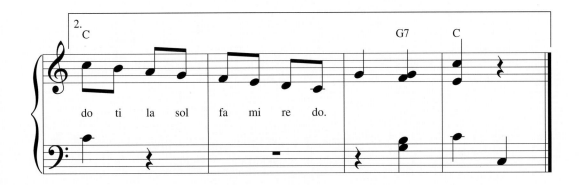

do   ti   la   sol   fa   mi   re   do.

The Sound of Music

Lyrics by OSCAR HAMMERSTEIN II
Music by RICHARD RODGERS

Moderately fast

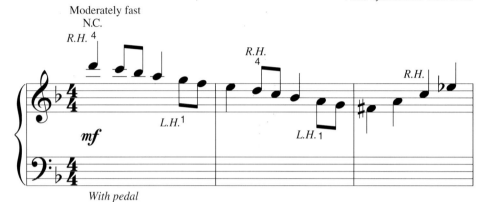

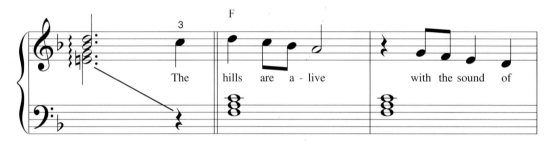

The hills are a-live with the sound of

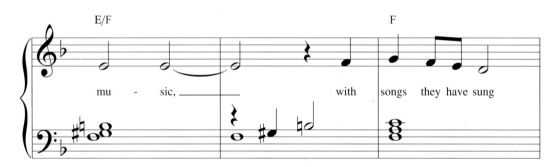

mu - sic, with songs they have sung

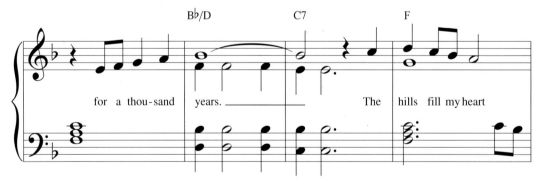

for a thou-sand years. The hills fill my heart

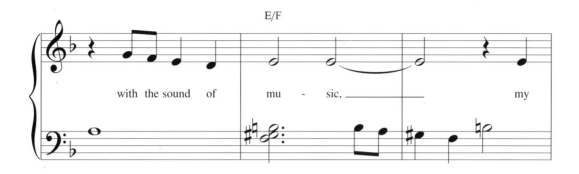

with the sound of mu - sic, _____ my

heart wants to sing ev-'ry song it hears. _____ My heart wants to

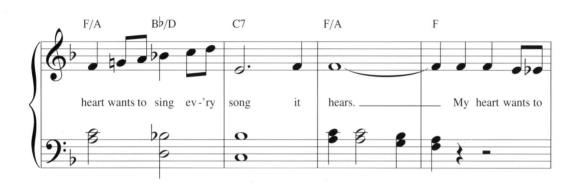

beat like the wings of the birds that rise from the lake to the

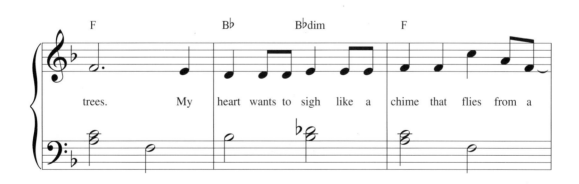

trees. My heart wants to sigh like a chime that flies from a

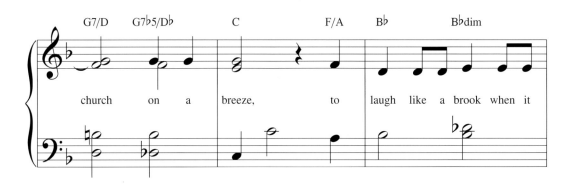

church   on   a   breeze,   to   laugh like a brook when it

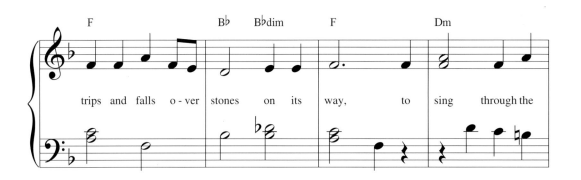

trips and falls o - ver stones   on   its   way,   to   sing   through the

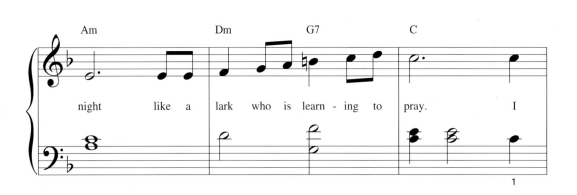

night   like a   lark who is learn - ing to   pray.   I

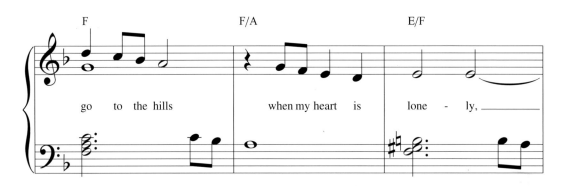

go   to the hills   when my heart is   lone -   ly, _____

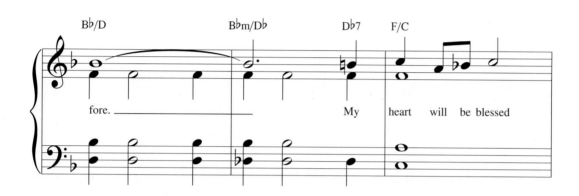

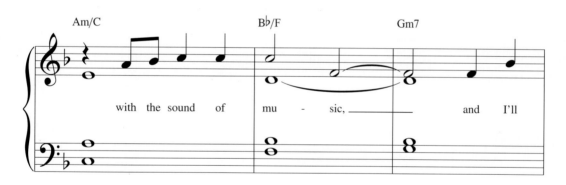

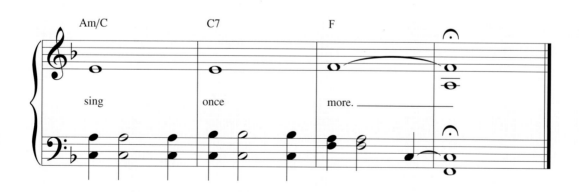

Wicked

Based on a novel by Gregory Maguire, with music and lyrics by Stephen Schwartz, *Wicked* is the story of Oz long before, and after, Dorothy's arrival. Two witches develop an unlikely friendship: Elphaba, smart, passionate, but misunderstood, and Galinda (Glinda), beautiful, determined, and very popular. They struggle with opposing viewpoints, romantic rivalry and the corrupt city of Oz on their way to becoming the Wicked Witch of the West and the Good Witch of the North. A favorite on Broadway and on tour, *Wicked* has broken box-office records around the world.

For Good

Music and Lyrics by
STEPHEN SCHWARTZ

Tenderly, poco rubato

With pedal

GLINDA: I've heard it said that peo-ple

come in-to our lives for a rea-son, _____ bring-ing

some-thing we must learn, and we are led to those who

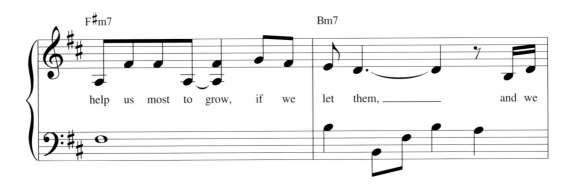

help us most to grow, if we let them, _____ and we

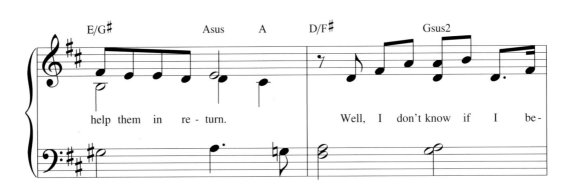

help them in re - turn. Well, I don't know if I be-

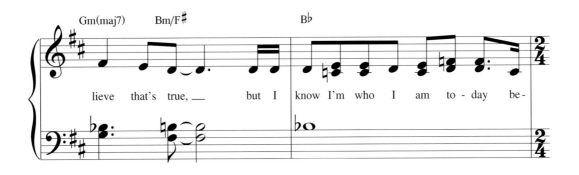

lieve that's true, ___ but I know I'm who I am to - day be-

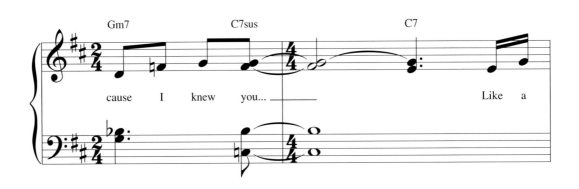

cause I knew you... _____ Like a

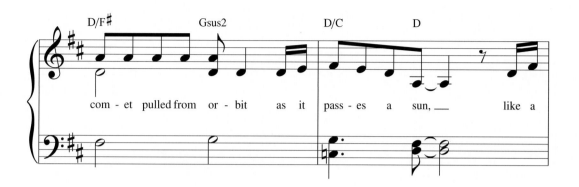

com - et pulled from or - bit as it pass - es a sun, ___ like a

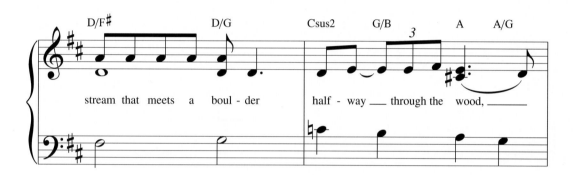

stream that meets a boul - der half - way ___ through the wood, ___

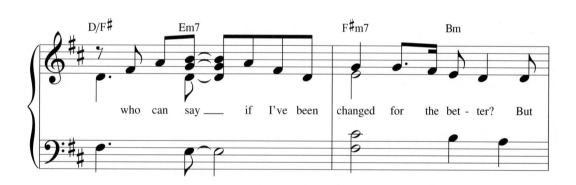

who can say ___ if I've been changed for the bet - ter? But

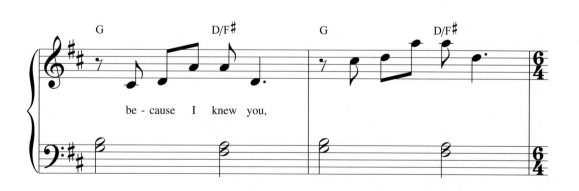

be - cause I knew you,

I have been changed for good.

It well may be that we will never meet again in this life-time, so let me say be-fore we part; so much of me is made of

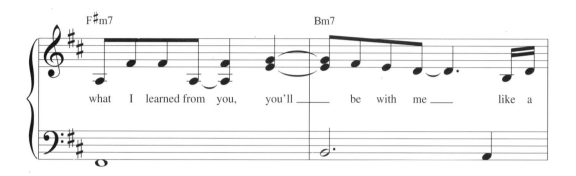

F#m7 ... Bm7

what   I   learned from you,   you'll _____   be with me _____   like a

E/G#   Asus   A   D/F#   Gsus2

hand - print   on   my   heart.   And   now   what - ev - er   way   our

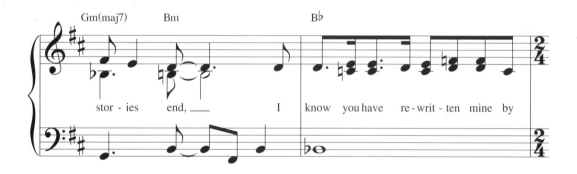

Gm(maj7)   Bm   Bb

stor - ies   end, _____   I   know   you have   re - writ - ten   mine   by

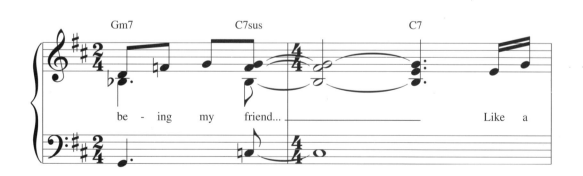

Gm7   C7sus   C7

be - ing   my   friend... _____   Like a

ship blown from its moor - ing by a wind off the sea, ____ like a

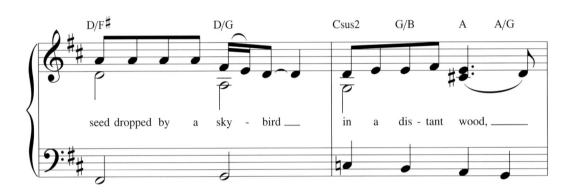

seed dropped by a sky - bird ____ in a dis - tant wood, _____

who can say ____ if I've ____ been changed for the bet - ter? But
dim.

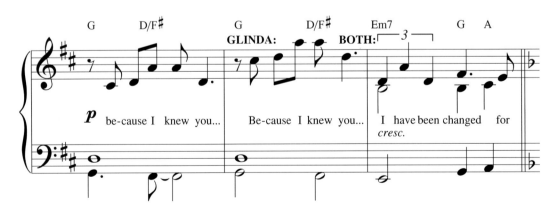

GLINDA: **BOTH:**

p be-cause I knew you... Be-cause I knew you... I have been changed for
cresc.

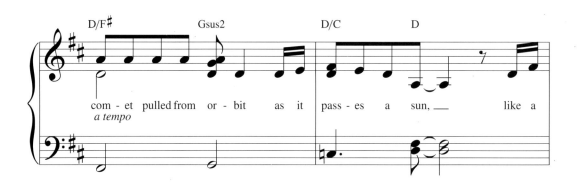

com - et pulled from or - bit as it pass - es a sun, ___ like a

a tempo

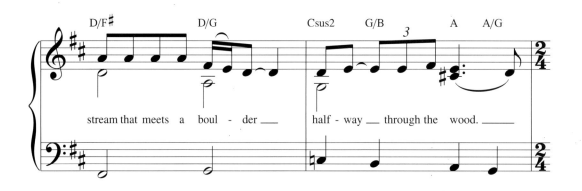

stream that meets a boul - der ___ half - way ___ through the wood. _____

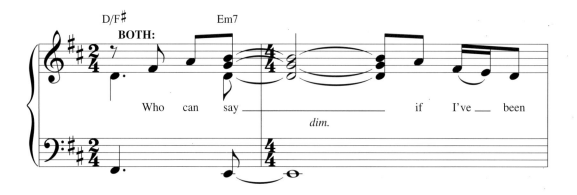

BOTH:

Who can say _____ if I've ___ been

dim.

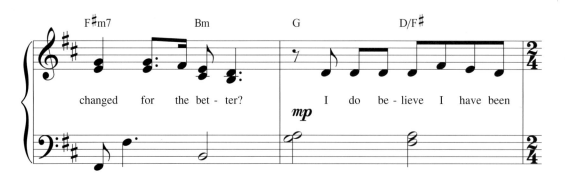

changed for the bet - ter? I do be - lieve I have been

mp

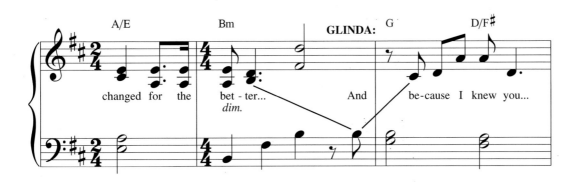

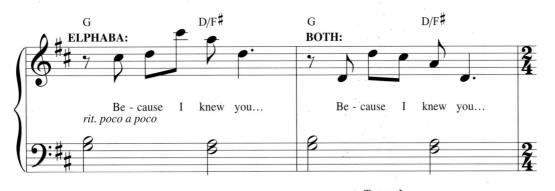

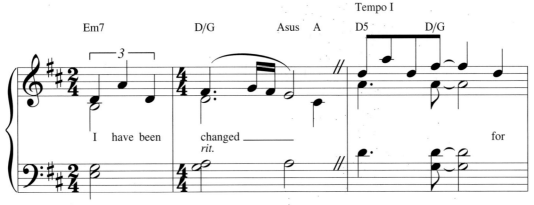

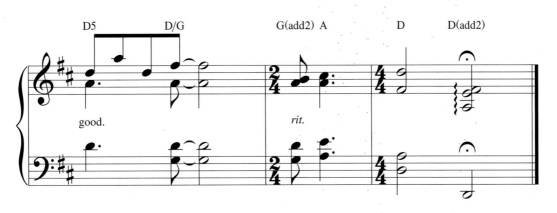

Defying Gravity

Music and Lyrics by
STEPHEN SCHWARTZ

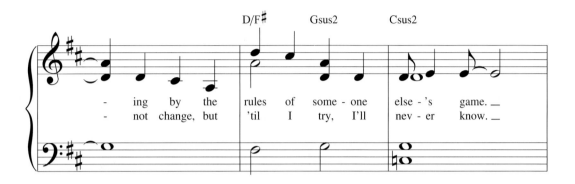

- ing by the rules of some - one else - 's game. __
- not change, but 'til I try, I'll nev - er know. __

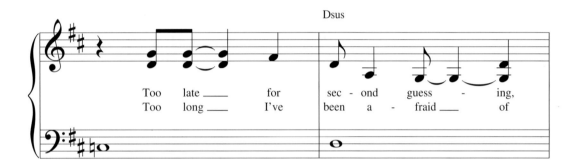

Too late __ for sec - ond guess - ing,
Too long __ I've been a - fraid __ of

too late to go back to sleep. __ It's time to
los - ing love I guess I've lost. __ Well, if that's

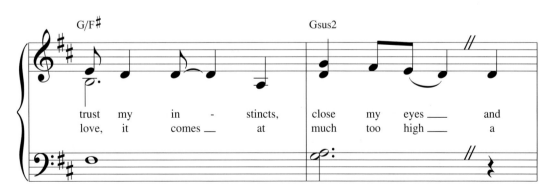

trust my in - stincts, close my eyes __ and
love, it comes __ at much too high __ a

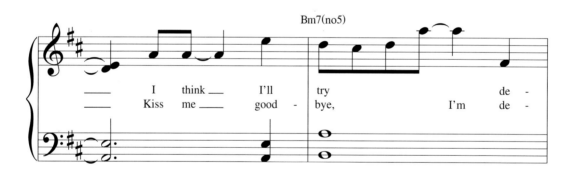

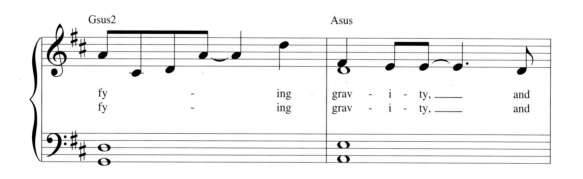

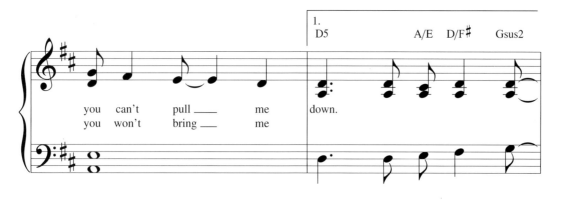

1.
D5 A/E D/F♯ Gsus2

you can't pull _____ me down.
you won't bring _____ me

D5 A/E D/F♯ Gsus2

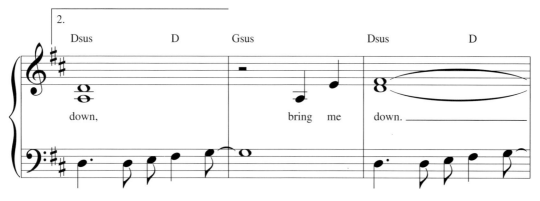

2.
Dsus D Gsus Dsus D

down, bring me down. _____

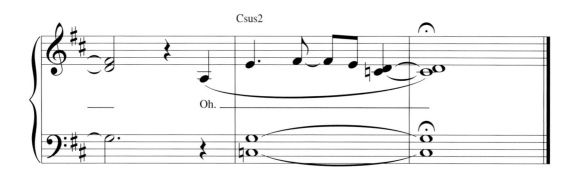

Csus2

Oh.